Saccharin and Plastic Band Aids
Comments in Poetic Prose

by Branch Isole

Saccharin and Plastic Band Aids
Comments in Poetic Prose
by Branch Isole

Printed in the United States of America

Library of Congress Control Number:
2004112916

ISBN 0974769282
ISBN 978-0974769288

Hampton, VA 23666

Order additional copies of this book at
www.manaopublishing.com

cover art; Tre Facce Oro
"Three Faces of Life" (Comedy, Tragedy, Rage)
by Leonardo da Vinci

The poems herein are poetic prose short stories
surrounding issues and emotions of personal
responsibility choice and avoidance.
They engage the reader in life situations often
experienced, but not always voiced.
This is 'Voyeurism Poetry'.

Voyeurism Poetry is purpose filled story telling
intended to paint images for the observer while
evoking responses of identity and reflection.

Saccharin and Plastic Band Aids contains
adult themes and language, some of which
is erotic or sexual in nature and presentation.
It is intended for mature audiences.

Contents

Angels
Avoidance
Beast of Burden
Boy Meats Girl
By A Nose
Carrots
Challenge
Comedian
Coming Out
Covering
Da Vinci Oversight
Doing Time
Dressing Down
Envy
For Adults Only
Freedom
Head Shots
I Wear, Therefore I am
Icons
Imperfect Balance
Internal Affair
Love Potion
Maybe
Missing You
Monkees, Terminators and Poltergeists
Moment Tarry Immediacy

Morning Pabulum
New Day
Next
Only Love
Open
Oral-Aural Addiction
Overweight
Partially Sage, Rose Married in Time
Penance
Penmanship
Planet Reality
PT 109
Rainbow
Recaptured Youth
Royal Highness
Sanguine Rivers
Sounds of Silence
Spilled Milk
Strutters
Tattoo
Tethered
The Box
Vegas Run
Wall Flower
We Three
Youth

Introduction

We live in a time when 'flash' has inevitably overtaken substance. The evolution of our post modern social experiment continues to be driven by imitation, in lieu of avant garde origination.

The side effects of our current tunnel vision will pay big dividends in our further demise as a society and people. Coupled with the future pain we can expect by dressing our festering wounds with Saccharin and Plastic Band Aids, the ills of our cultural hemorrhage will only become more exacerbated.

It won't be the disease that kills us.
It will be our misconstrued belief that we can manipulate the truth and outwit the parameters of life's lessons with its innate natural processes.

Branch Isole

“So often times it happens
that we live our lives in chains
and we never even know
we have the key.”

-J Tempchin/R. Stradlund-
from “Already Gone”
‘Eagles Their Greatest Hits 1971-1975’

Angels

We're biker bad
and sport a look
An image designed
to keep civvies shook

Our trademarks;
leathers
skulls and wings
the number 13
and of course
Milwaukee's own
Harley D,
homage all
to Sonny B.

No Far East
sewing machine engines for us
Before we ride those
we'll take the bus

We've battled long
We've battled hard
from state to state to state
With governments we've pleaded please,
as to helmet laws
don't legislate
Leave our MVA induced epilepsy
and head trauma injuries
to God and fate

We ride from here to there
to Sturgis,
Laughlin
everywhere
We gather, meet and party
each year across the land
From two's and three's
to thousands
we're an outlaw riding clan

We've been labeled
and called a gang,
of rebels
misfits
and thugs
Making our family
just like yours,
different individuals
each full of love

We live to ride
and ride to live
claiming all the while
We alone are riding free
and all the while
we live as you,
in group conformity

(MVA - Motor Vehicle Accidents,
Sonny B. - Ralph "Sonny" Barger;
founder of Hell's Angels Motorcycle Club)

Avoidance

God, How Great Thou Art
that you would use your awesome powers
to allow each of us to live on
and be in your presence eternally,
merely by believing in you
and recognizing your Spirit
in the one you sent
Our way of reconciliation
Our redeemer thwarting death
Our councilor of wisdom
A mediator for our sinfulness

Awareness of our spirit within
living forever
is beyond our imagination
It is an understanding impossible for us to grasp
in its sublime enormity

We who live from moment to moment
day to day
counting the years
as if they were capsules of permanence
in which to invest

Overlooking your purpose for each.
To come closer to the blessings you offer
for obedience and belief.
You ask nothing more of us
and yet,
we spend life's time and energy
finding all manner of excuse
to avoid you and your word

Beast of Burden

Bending
Pulled at the waist
sprained lumbar muscles ache
Pressure bearing down
upon strained shoulders that tire

The weight of bulging
plastic bags
brimming with goods
brandishing red tags
lining forearms in a row
like birds upon a wire

Taut tendons
attempt to hold perpendicular
exhausted arms that ever-so-slightly sag
As ninety degrees
increasingly becomes
one-forty-three

Loaded on both sides
as if a beast of burden
packing in provisions
a full season's supply
That life might be extended
through the cold cruel winter
pending the arrival
of nature's rejuvenating spring?

No,
just another day at the mall
searching out the saleables
Buying more
for it is there
and ever so available

There still being
a vacuous four feet
in a garage designed for two cars
One is nestled
against the curb at the street
the other, parked on the yard

Spending money
yet to be made
living on the come
Anticipating, Salivating
over next week's
next month's
next sale
When on the shelves
there will be more
to pack in from the stores

Jackass

Boy Meats Girl

Hurt me
Restrain me
Stomp me
with your stiletto heels
Damn, you're sexy
in leather and lace
Besmirched 'pearl necklace'
across your face

Ambivalence never once entered
their bed
their couch
nor kitchen floor
Even with his stake in her mouth
Her back against
the Frigidaire door

Breaking free
from nylon stockings that bind
Hostage now predator
as tables are turned
Revenge and mayhem
on her mind

Our dominance role played to a "T"
it was one hellacious
exciting trip
Reflectively watching
acting free
as both got off, on
the whip, grip

Peeping through the keyhole
mesmerized by your touch
of self
With a smile so coy
eyeing secret toys
waiting on the shelf

Imagining mind's fantasies
playing, played out
in new sex games
of bottom and top
Knowing once the friction starts
it's haltingly hard
for a feigned cuckold assault to stop

Barking out commands
riding deep from behind
Screams declare
one's coming soon
As a howl is loosed
at an exposed pale moon

The force of lustful love
exhausting
screwed and bent
Two together totally spent

Salivating
Dreaming
Scheming
Tongue licking
Major and minor lip kissing

Hungered arousal
re-building

Sex starved lovers
crescendo re-rising

By A Nose

What is it that propels us
to lean forward
that we might break the tape
and be revered
in the eyes of men

In our youth
it was a sense of accomplishment
bound up in efforts to try
The enjoyment we gained
from participation sufficient
there being no prize
Other than respite filled reminiscing
after clashing with combative foes
Until time and situation
presented our next meeting,
again to be tested on the field of endeavor

Win or lose
it was in the post locked eyes of competitors
revealing a shared sense of
"I enjoyed doing my best"
where inner satisfaction was found

We reveled in our opponent's
momentary success over our own
as much as they did ours
For we were comrades in the struggle
Opposition fed life into the opportunity

It became organized.
We believed, becoming fiercer.
The wound was opened
and the salt of provincial pride poured in

We lean further to break the tape
in the light of cameras flashing
and to the calls of commercial endorsement

Carrots

Faustian carrots dangle
Frustrations assimilate
Osmotic mixed metaphor signals
Barbs press from every degree
of the compass rose
their maelstrom briar prevalence
as within a thicket

Nowhere to turn
Nor a moment's peace

Decades swirl past
Chronology blurs

Each spectral test;
self
versus perceived self
in light's shadow
of planned outcome self

Image imagined
imagination fertile,
producing . . .
the next carrot;
different color
size, shape, status, value

Evidence,
someone will notice

at what cost?
for whom?
why?

Proving to ourselves
we were here

Challenge

Up for a challenge
Post-modern man?. . . .
Try bringing this life style
under your command;
Common sense
in choice, action, direction
Attempt truth as your foundation

No heralding trumpets needed
announcing your entrance
be heeded
Your identity crisis insecurities
are proudly pleaded
by your corporeal
tattoos, piercings,
and prevaricating publicly heard
private cell phone conversations

Comedian

Voltaire had it right
when he nailed your act
describing your audience "too afraid to laugh"
delivering one liners
because you can and so choose

tossing airborne your two sided coinage
watching it float, teetering on edge
false sense of endearment
fear of retribution, which will it be
our outstretched arms strain over the ledge

beat docile and frightened
fragility keeps us pegged
as pachyderm to the stump
we hold all the cards
lest one of course
yours, always, mega-trump

all this because you didn't want to be alone
all this to ensure throngs before your throne
you create
you plan
you design
each niche
why so often do your three monty efforts
appear as bait and switch

Coming Out

Is this the day,
the day I come out,
come out of the closet?

Is today the day,
the day I reveal to the world
I am and have been
for as long as I can remember
Homosexual,
Gay
Queer
Fag
Pansy
Dandy. . .
There, I've said it

What about you
Pharisaic Christian?
Is my speck so great
you can't see
your plank of hypocrisy,
Shall it just fade away?

Now to climb
the highest steeple
and openly declare
to every person
to all people

I'm out
I'm finally out
I haven't changed
I'm not deranged
It's still me
Let me be free

Free to live my life
To love who I am
and who I will
All I ask
is you let me choose,
just as I allow
you to do

What about you
Church Age Christian?
Is my speck so great
you can't see
your plank of dogma,
Shall it just fade away?

I'm aware of what the Bible says
Did *you* miss the part
where in His sight,
a sin is a sin

I'll let God be my judge
and put me in my place
when I see Him
face to face

What about you
Carnal Christian?
Is my speck so great
you can't see
your plank of self-righteousness,
Shall it just fade away?

Covering

Night after night
Listening to singers
each eve of the week
Different styles, different look
changes of latitude
changes in attitude,
yet each sings cover
right from the book

Night after night
These patrons don't care
they're drinking and talking
saving this time in a bottle,
hustling, flirting with one another
imbibing their own brand of cheer

Night after night
The singer believes
it's all about him
they've been coming to see,
A mini concert
he's ready to give
prepared to live vicariously,
as Joel or Buffet
Nelson or Croce

Night after night
Not one of his own
penned or recorded
none can he claim
Touring dreams and accolades
of being on the road again
to riches, possessions
and most of all fame

Night after night
He sings cover
imitating others
who've gone before
Retired, dead
or now passé
soon he too
will be one day

Night after night
He dreams and struggles
screams and juggles
cover, after cover, after cover

Years of cover imitation
of lifestyle anticipation
still beyond his reach
He has yet to learn
originals are priceless
and copies
three cents each

Da Vinci Oversight

Leonardo watches,
overseeing flying fingers
and stuttered thoughts
As if ready to speak
while gazing at writer and words
simultaneously

An approving nod
A piqued smile
Waiting unhurried
upon one or the other
He simply stares
at the work being developed

A postmodern rendition
of his own Mona Lisa-esque stature
artist becomes subject
fawned to for inspiration

One
with Jesus and Lennon
A triumvirate of mind, spirit and soul

Doing Time

Within this life
we all pick our poison
our style
We get an inch
and take a mile
We look for an omen
and pray for a sign,
in this reality
we're all doing time

Whether ensnared
by body
or trapped
by mind
the truth is,
we're all doing time

Obesity,
so real it hurts
dreaming of mini skirts
One more piece of that cream pie,
she's just doing time

Embarrassing shame
of sexual abuse
Torn between feelings
so good, so bad
plays with and pains the mind,
he's just doing time

Whether ensnared
by body
or trapped
by mind
the fact is,
we're all doing time

In debt up to here
living with creditor
phone call fears
Please oh please
five little lotto numbers in a line,
you're just doing time

Needles and spoons
and one-hundred proof
they all say
I act aloof,
funny thing is
I don't notice them
is that a crime?
I'm just doing time

Entangled by a schizophrenic mind
crazy, homeless
no yarn on the spool
Maybe later
they'll get help too
after the triplicate paperwork is signed
meanwhile,
they're just doing time

Whether ensnared
by body
or trapped
by mind,
we're all doing time

The bars may be gold, 24 karat
or iron
platinum
straw or hay
No matter their make up
they're each cold as steel
and each makes
the caged to feel
as if their life
is somehow surreal
like celluloid; reel to reel

Others get the dollars
while you get the dime
that's how far
you are behind
until you recognize,
we're all doing time

Dressing Down

Looking is free
It feeds our fantasies
Eager to show us your outside
too much of you
is voluntarily exposed

There are reasons for the amount
of you, you've chosen to reveal
Casting hooks of desirability
you wish us to want to feel
If there was more
of less of you
you longed for us to see
you wouldn't be dressing
down,
so provocatively

Don't indignantly glare
down,
at us
your nose elevated in the air
You're the one dressing
down
Evidence of your insecurities
laid publicly bare

The extent to which
you put forth
as mitigating proof
Is it time to view introspectively
the exhibition of your self doubting game
as simple truth and dare

Envy

It is in our nature
to emulate
and upon a pedestal
to separate
those to whom
we look and gaze
through a duplicitous
myopic
idyllic haze,
and do we idolize
from afar
those we label,
"star"

Unknowing that beneath
a thin veneer
hidden from adoring eyes
are stored the remains
and caches of pain
under unhealed scars

Many a hearts
been broken
and dreams world wide
been shattered
When our hero's humanity
is nakedly exposed
and their iconic image
is left maimed and battered

The mask of celebrity lifted
The veil of pomposity drawn back
Alone in the spotlight left to burn
before inquisitors
do they twist and turn
The objects of our devotion
hanging to the glee of catcalls
while it is our emotions
which choke and squirm

It is we who suffer
the slings and arrows
whereby we bleed their pain
As a carnivorous world
tears apart and laughs,
and we look inward
to discover
the unrealistic expectations
we have purposed upon them,
were on our own behalf

For Adults Only

Noticed a woman drinking water today
from a plastic bottle
with a pull spout nipple

How conveniently apropos
that Twenty-First Century denizens
of mental will and wit
can still partake
the sense and sensation
of being on the teat

Saw an advertisement today
dispensing an informative repartee
for a more dependable adult diaper
they did say

From infant, to macro infant
the reality of our advancement made
is beginning to reach its potential,
its recognizable zenith
and simultaneous retrograde

As the world of commerce
enjoys product rebirths
inevitably cast
on the backsides and wallets
of Baby Boomers
while collecting increasing amounts of mass
acceptance

No wonder so many
in this neo-post modern age
refuse to grow up

Freedom

As muse
you supply a peace
allowing freedom
from all intruding thoughts

Head Shots

Three faces have I,
one for public
one for private
one for all my lies

There's one
for official legaldom;
licenses, passports, decrees
Another with airbrushed vanity
for those piqued by sex to see
The third is kept
under wraps
in a law enforcement dossier
A mug shot if there ever was,
epitome of a truly bad hair
and sallow pale skin day

A secreted past
determines which
I choose to use on you,
selecting the persona
that fits like a glove;

hateful
indifferent
indecisive

comforting
compassionate
full of love

Interested in flash?
My public smile you'll see
Look ever more closely
at these private eyes
beneath levels of ocular peel
behind each layer is revealed
deeper insecurities

What of the third? you ask,
Enquiring minds want to know
Where substance of character
ought to dwell,
honesty eludes
truthfulness evades
morality is quelled

Shackled and bound
tied in lies
enslaved by self-deceit
Life's theater masks
'Comic, Rage and Tragic'
sweet and sour replete
Maims not the world
yet stains and pierces
the liar's ego armored shell

I Wear, Therefore I am

It's been said,
"we are what we eat"
Today however
it's more likely to be
the thoughts and ideas
we believe and share
are on our favorite T-shirts
that we wear

For many their chest worn mastheads
loudly proclaim them to be
Part
drone
or proponent of
a mega-corporate identity

Others declare a place
they've been or seek to be
if not today, tomorrow
if at all possible to see
Definitely this year
or the next
once they've saved
additional eggs in the nest

Lest we forget the multitude of others
with emblazoned emblematic jerseys
ensconced with number identities
those maniacal sports devotees
Or those showing blatantly arrogant
skulls, whips and chains
spouting blood splattered sayings
of desires promulgating decay

There are not many shirts
about God and country,
Mom and Pop
unless they be done in jest
Nor few proverbial learned statements
with encouragement to do one's best
Why in the world sacrifice retail space
away from all the rest

It's enlighteningly more informative
eyeing sex laden graphics that glare
depicting what's most important
in the life of the wearer
Especially those
who voluntarily crow
about "Woody's" and "Johnson's"
and other dildo innuendo

Patiently waiting
for the coming day
when from a store
a lone body strays
wearing a clean
and laundered 'T'
with a printed definition of humility

Icons

Plastic Jesus
on my dash
Stoic Ben Franklin
on my cash

To a Madonna
do I pray
Ciccone, six nights
Mother Mary, Sunday

Brothers K, three did fall
Their pictures still adorn my wall
Lone conspirator's bullet did fly
My government would never lie

Church leaders
Men of God
self purported righteous styles?
Nay.
corrupters
liars, deceivers,
ecclesiastic pedophiles

Who will finance
our next 'Prez' golden?
To which moneyed group
will he be beholden?
From two fields of liars
connivers
and cheats
Who will be chosen
to protect our streets?

Enron Lays
World Com Ebbers
Imclone Sams
and Marthas
To hear their side
they had it rough
Fleeced investors ask
when is enough, enough ?

Tip of the berg
A teapot tempest
to skirt the truth
they do their damnedest

Wall Street's cycle
cycles of greed
upon their clients
these piranhas do feed
Either way
boom or bust
It matters not
just abuse the trust

A cinematic winner
above competitive fray?
Hollywood Blockbuster!
(at least for one day)

Lousy plot,
Acting? Not!
Story? Characters?
Wish one would
Wish one could
The movie stinks,
but the trailer was good

Who needs dialogue
or characters played
when two hours of special effects
have been made
America's Idol,
You mean, this week?
To recall one prior
would be a real feat

Instant fame,
today's name of the game
"I've made it to twenty-three
time to write my autobiography"

Soup Can Andy
rolls over in his grave
'15 minutes'
down to this moment's naïve

Imperfect Balance

There is only one
who delights in our sin
more than we,
and that is the Devil himself

To him
the bitter aftertaste
of our guilt
is as sweet
as the anticipation
of our own unrepentant commitment

When we rebel
against the moral directives
of the Lord
the further our separation
from God becomes

Unable to establish
perfect balance between the two
We are ever moving
closer to one
and farther from the other

Internal Affair

First we kissed
then we touched
then more
oh so much

The sex was hot
The guilt was not
Thoughts,
of getting caught
for doing things
that we ought not

I believe I was
as nervous as he,
although it was left
for me to lead

I don't know why
or what made me do it
Honestly,
I'm not sure
I'm not a bad person
(*really*)
Nor a sexual predator
(*I don't believe*)

Was it boredom,
insecurity
self-serving desires?
That he was young
and available
or worse,
that he was easy to control
and coerce?

What started out
as a flirting game
between two well known strangers
turned ugly and soon,
too soon
was fraught with too much danger

Sneaking around
was half the fun,
until my husband discovered
I was fucking his son

Love Potion

Thank you Lord for all you do in my life
My desire is that you would prod me
closer to you
for it is there, with you
fulfillment of my heart is accomplished

Knowing it is not in your nature
nor your design to force
you allow us each to interact with you
of our own free will,
to be closer to you . . .
Or not

Maybe

Daddy,
After breakfast?
Maybe

After lunch?
Maybe

After dinner?
Maybe

After the hike?
Maybe

After the beach?
Maybe

After the game?
Maybe

After school?
Maybe

On Saturday?
Maybe

After church?
Maybe

Well,
What did he say?
He said 'No'

Missing You

May the love we share
Grow stronger each day
And never ever
Pass away

For we love as two,
Loving as one
We love each other
As He and His Son

Whether near or far
It matters not
Like a thief in the night
By your love I've been caught

By your love
Your glances
Caress and touch
Your kiss
Your words
Of these I can't get enough

for CC

Monkees, Terminators and Poltergeists

"They're Back"

"Here they come
walking down the street"
the Californicators bellowing
'it's all about me'

Here come the Californicators
batten down the hatches
Their pandemic offensive antics
upon local populations
are about to be loosed
Even women and children
will be exposed to egomaniacal tirades
and unending cell phone abuse

Here come the Californicators
using monikers like
"the O C "
What the hell is that?
An abbreviated behavior disorder
or a side effect
from too much TV?

Here come the Californicators
putting on a show
exhibiting how rich they really aren't
trying every trick in the book
to prove it just ain't so

Here come the Californicators
please God help us out once more
there's no telling what this season
they will have in store
Rudeness
Crudeness
Silicone galore
Overexposed tattooed skin
flailing on every shore

Here come the Californicators
Do they say please and thank you,
dude?
"No way, Jose"
they're too busy thong parading
running around half nude

Here come the Californicators
"well Excussse meeee"
like "It's all good"
like "I'm driving here"
"like we're from Cali
here to play
you don't got no right o' way"

Here come the Californicators
toting around heir hordes
of misanthropic progeny
to every part of town
Leaving in ruins
handling and destroying
everything not nailed down

Here come more Californicators
arriving day and night
As others leave on jet planes
singing in a chorus
on each departing flight

"You island homies think
'Maui No Ka Oi'
means 'Maui is the best'
Starting next season
it will mean,
Maui . . .
the 'O C West' "

"We'll Be Back"

Moment Tarry Immediacy

Difficulties do exist
Experiencing particular moments

Worries about the future
Reminiscing on the past
Thought filled conundrums occupy
our perception of 'now'

Living 'now'
appears as a flash
caught threadbare
between two great glaciers of grey;
time and space

The arrival of
moment tarry immediacy
catches us off guard

"Oh, that moment?
It came and went. . .
thinking I was ready,
I missed it"

And so it goes
Moment by moment
Day to day
Lifetime slipping away

Morning Pabulum

We're *Number One*!
when it comes to the News
This the network mantra
cackled boastfully today
by more than a few

At least five media news organizations
declared their ratings supremacy
Not being a Gallup nor a Nielsen
I won't dispute
what they have to say

In meeting viewers needs however
I question their intent
It appears to be more
about talking heads
than about the audience

All I glean
as a morning viewer
coffee cup in hand,
is early morning news programs
are not much more than bland

It's gone so far beyond hum drum
most of what they spew
is no longer news
it's a.m. TV pabulum

Give me the news
or get me two Tums
Your servings of mush
gives my head the runs

A story about a three legged dog
Another about saving a log
Did you see the one about the gear and cog
Or concern over a newly drained bog

When it's terror, murder
or mayhem, sure
they're all quick to jump
But a story about two office clerks
officially naming a day, "hump?"
Which investigative journalist managed
to uncover those two jerks?

Give me the news
or get me two Tums
Your servings of pabulum
gives my brain the runs

On at least one occasion today
each network has claimed to own
the coveted news top spot
In our hyper media world however
being newsworthy and professional
seems to be at odds
more often than not

There's way too much
precious time to fill
with twenty-four/seven programming needs
and in today's News of the World,
if it bleeds, it leads

Give me the news
or get me two Tums
Your servings of pabulum
gives my mind the runs

Making every mole hill story
into a mountainous event
with continuous live ongoing coverage
leaves me totally spent

Its true importance
in the scheme of things
is obvious because tomorrow,
after today's 'Big Story' has hit the airwaves
that with which we could not live without
is now on the cutting room floor
or archived in the waste basket
behind the newsroom door

New Day

Welcome to the world, I say
Welcome to the world, it's another new day
Welcome to the world, I see
Another new day smiling down on me.

Next

Drama
concerning inconsequential things

Bipolar behavior
expressed as if mental acuity
and personality growth
had been blockaded at age fifteen

Narcissistic blinders
prompt and restrict
resulting in tunnel vision swings
wildly,
from one pendulum extreme to the other
testing reactions to responses of
satiate me,

no,
hate me

Emotional insanity on the rise
covered by a thin disguise
"it's all good" even if I'm not
I'm relying on you
for my next thought

I can't be responsible
for what I think, do or say
then there would be consequences
from which I can't run away

Believing "we loved
'beyond forever' " one day
knowing each other twenty minutes
this profession we made

Voluminous traits in common
ink, holes, eighth grade,
peripherally the perfect match
dysfunctional core, nuclear baggage
making complete our long eluded catch

Yes there have been others
numerous ones it's true
but we have managed substitutes
each moment the last is through,
the issue, basic
self evidently exposed
solid foundations crumble
from tremors of clarity
the minute either of us
takes our eyes off of me

Only Love

There is Only Love,
no other wellspring of emotion exists
Only Love

for even he
or she
full of hate,

loves to hate

Open

Open my mind Lord
that it might be filled with you
Open my heart
that it might be filled anew.
Open my eyes Lord
to see the truth
Open my arms
that they might receive a hint of you.
Open my shell Lord
to release my soul
Let my spirit fly through your universe whole.
Open my essence Lord and let it be
Allow me to serve
your name eternally.

Oral-Aural Addiction

I'm a cell phone junkie
I can't get enough
My earlobes have cartilage nodules
from conversing too much

My tele-com company makes it easy
for me to stay in touch
talking about those
in my life,
the ones I despise so much

Yes, the contract
is many months long
and they continue to raise my rates,
but I can't bear missing out
on all those egos
and their dubious fates

I'm an addict
of oral-aural stimulation
as my mind attempts to process
this love-hate integration

I enjoy hearing it
seeing it
on my video phone
but ever more
without my cellular fix
my life is such a bore

Kudos to those tele-com
cellular engineers
They've enabled me to broadcast
my insecure fears
worldwide to my friends,
both of them

I'd like to stop
but "No" I can't say
Bad news for me
but good news for tele-com revenue coffers,
and the NSA

(NSA - National Security Agency)

Overweight

One hundred fifty plus pounds
of physical inertia
compresses claustrophobically
every segment of being
snaring the spirit beneath,
cutting off all routes of escape, save one
death

Only will liberation of the soul
allow the spirit
to regain its rightful place in the cosmos
awaiting rebirth
Until then,
the trap set
the quarry captured
soul and spirit smothered
beneath blood and flesh

Gagged by thoughts of here and now
Overwhelmed by outside influences
Keeping freedom held at bay
Cognition, light years distance away

Ignited by a spark of unconscious awareness
and fueled by inexplicable innate knowledge
of priori existential presence,
what once was
shall one day
be again

Partially Sage, Rose Married in Time

If you want to be a better husband
listen to your wife
If you want to be a better father
listen to your wife
If you want to be a better man
listen to your wife
If you want to have a better life,
listen to your wife

Penance

She goes to her knees and feels helpless
The motivation heartfelt
The action embarrassing
Would that her desire be fulfilled
by this movement
yet in doing so she feels at once
guilt ridden,
so her shame keeps her seated
as conflict between her need to acquiesce
and her choice of not moving
keeps her farther from him

She remembers examples set forth
in words and pictures
They spring to life
as two dimensional images
vivid in memory's mind
as if reality recalled

Taught the guidance reward
received by him
she too might share
a transcendent moment of peace,
yet still she sits
unable to reconcile mentally the emotion
whereby a similar action itself
condemns her sinfulness

The battle line drawn
between cognition and surrender
she realizes again
his forgiving patience and understanding

Without a single word
nor one prepared
she kneels in prayer,
and he draws closer

Penmanship

Cutting our teeth
on words which came before
Utterances and vocabulary
scribed by masters
far and near

From across the timeline
of literary history
their words and phrases so rich, so clear

Unlike our musical brethren
we, unable to initialize
nay replicate, acceptable cover
in order to practice and hone
our fledgling efforts as bards

Imitation in art, flattery
For the poet, the writer;
plagiaristic battery

How can the poet's work
so brief yet fully concise
attempt to convey
beginning, middle and end
within each separate piece
freshly penned

Planet Reality

Bound and gagged
struggling to be free
Free to be
just to be me
Go along with the world
it'll be ok
Standing in line
day after day
No marching to
a different drum
"we'll have to put a stop
to your wagging tongue"

It's our way, or no way
That's what they say

It's true
they are opposed to me
but only by
one hundred eighty degrees
I may be wrong . . .
but I may be right
when it comes to this particular fight

Not bending to PC conformity
Nor bound to corpus identity

It's our way, always our way
That's what they say

What we learn
is what we are told
What we know
is what we are sold
Kept in darkness, blinded by light
Unexposed to truth, retreating from its sight

Those who claim to want to lead
keep their followers from being freed
Sharing forms of their vanity
through vicarious moments of insanity

It's our way, or the highway
That's what they say

What is your way going to be?
What will you do
if you're ever set free?

Today's victims' song
"we've been wronged"
An alphabet disorder
To level the field, to make it fair
To help take each, from here to there

'Tis a solo journey
which we endure
constantly looking
for a common cure,
cures for all ills
in the form of their pills

What is your way going to be?
Where will you go
if you're ever set free?

We put our sights
on things we desire
praying,
we will never tire
of the commerce in this world
to which we are tied
gathering more and more
before we die

Our goals, our ambitions
our blood, sweat and tears
Designed to calm
our growing fears
Fears of today, fears of tomorrow
Why else do we
beg, steal and borrow?

Again and again
from beginning to end
on waves of totality
our voyages in reality

What is your way going to be?
How will you know
when you're finally free?

From whence did we come
and where are we bound
Spirit made flesh
returned to the ground

PT 109

I've heard the men here at work
talk of your beguiling ways
surely you recognize
the label they've bestowed
and what they have to say

They call you 'PT 109'
branding every man
you've tested and teased
a member of JFK's sunken boat
You do to them so mercilessly
while each gets nothing from you
fueling opportunities for you to gloat

Observing as you operate,
at the water cooler
in the conference room
near the parking lot gate
Your moves and gestures
beyond belief
each as smooth as silk
How brilliantly
you make it clear
in no uncertain terms,
an affirmative response
forthcoming from you
will be as opaque as milk

You keep them jumping
and on their toes
You lead each around
by the ring in his nose
You keep them wondering
who might be cast
as the one,
the next,
the best,
your last

It's apparent each one new
will end up among the others,
piled high
upon the heap
discarded and labeled "past due"

It's interesting
and quite amusing
to watch your climbing skills
Ascending higher
the corporate ladder
leaving each valiant knight
in his shining armor
tarnished
and a little sadder

Many have become
what's deem 'gun shy'
Not at all eager
to compete for you
Most now anxious
not even to try

That left me wondering
if you please
what in the world will you do?
When none are left
to string along, Prick Tease
Your reputation, as it now precedes
pre-announcing your manipulative needs

Then it suddenly dawned on me
while watching you interact
It's not the men
you really want
It's the envy of all
those other women
who talk behind your back

Rainbow

Gazing across fields
of green topped cane
Ominously hovering
above Pacific blue waters
Gun metal grey clouds
and west pushing rain
Rapidly advance toward
island lands
as if a runaway train

Thrashed by high winds
descending in sheets
Rain's landfall bound steering
now complete

First drops strike,
single large splats
pelting hard
on safety glass

Cane bends low
touching the grass
under the windward strain
Paying honor to nature's
impending rain

Sudden deluge
hailing down
of sky's rushing fallout
As if the floodgates of heaven
had opened up their spouts

Wipers on high
not enough,
Visibility naught
in this downpour
we're caught

Only one thing
left to do
pull off the road now
and wait it out,
wait until
this rain is pau

First line's assault
passes quickly
moving up slope
to Pukalani

As close as a shadow
moisture combines
with rays of sunlight
creating a rainbow
of majestic kine

From Sugar Beach
to OGG's
longest runway reach
Maui's central valley now engulfed
by prism's colorful spectrum hues
From left to right
an unbelievable sight
this day seen by a relative few

(Pau [pronounced Pow] is Hawaiian for 'finished'.

Pukalani [pronounced Poo Ka Lawn Ee] is a Maui community located on the side of Haleakala [pronounced Ha Lee Ah Ka La] East Maui's volcano mountain.

OGG is the FAA/OAG designation for Maui's airport located in Kahului [pronounced Ka Hoo Lew Ee]

Kine as in 'Da Kine' a placeholder in Hawaiian Pidgin meaning 'anything' or 'everything' usually referring to "the best")

Recaptured Youth

The media is my god
Telling me
what to do
think
and say
Selling me insignificant
make-believe dream roles
to incessantly crave and portray

Trying, trying
to play a part
with no script
little experience
and sans-a-heart

Imitating purveyors
of the latest trend or fad
Living this insane lifestyle
without going mad

If retro time travel
is out of the question
and surgery too expensive
to mention,
What's a girl
ever to do?
Declare suicidally,
"I'm through"

Recaptured youth,
that's all I want
to be seventeen
and once more to flaunt
my Lolita innocence
and ignorance
of who I am, not

Back again
Back to when
I know I knew it all
To be who I believe
and think I can
Not,
who I truly am

Being brave
Being bold
Not a lost and insecure
thirty-eight year old

Royal Highness

Two people live
behind your mask
One mean
The other nasty,
What a task

To hold in abeyance
To hold in check
The energy it takes
to keep them reigned in
must take its toll
must make you a wreck

Each awaiting opportunity
at the end of your short fuse
Their catalyst
Temper,
Lit when self perception reveals
you've been attacked
questioned or used

Their purpose to triumph
at any and all costs
To show who's right
To defend your position
To win every fight

Both at the ready
Though when they are here
Your facile facade
unsteady,
unclear
Personal revenge
born of perceived betrayal
causes either or both
in your defense to rail

For an appearance
by either
or both it is true
you certainly pay a great cost
For the longer they stay
the further you stray
and the more your reality lost

Sanguine Rivers

non sequitur questions plagued him
as he stared blankly
while drawing the bath
and making ready

lowering his eyes
held in a trance
by the newly opened wound,
he watched the viscous red stream
flow into the hot water
at a steady rate
as if being pumped
from the depths of a bilge

the cut so clean
very little seepage
from surface capillaries was evident,
this precise incision
would serve its purpose
completing the task
in but a few reconnoitered minutes

half submerged
a womb-like calm
overtook him,
his body finally relaxing
from the tension of previous
anxiety ridden moments

he allowed himself
to supine fully,
the blood draining out,
the upturned corners of his lips
revealing a sinister smile

he repeated to himself
in a subconscious voice
'the blood draining out'
"which of course, it is"
he whispered aloud
as if in an unfinished conversation
with another

"not that it matters now"
he muttered almost incoherently,
their bodies 'lying in state'
so to speak
in the bedroom

weary,
he saw the mechanism's buttons
"ah" he droned, "a Jacuzzi"
that would speed up the process
but just as that statement and image
trailed off together
from his lips and brain
orated to no one in particular,
the self inflicted second wound
on his left wrist gaped open
additional blood flowing into the tub,
changing the water's color
from Pink Chablis
to a deeper hued Rosé

with a final thought,
“you can’t hurt me anymore”
he closed his eyes
and slipped into darkness

Sounds of Silence

If you ever want to see
or hear the sounds of silence
watch a tree sway in the breeze
and hear the wind chimes chiming

Spilled Milk

I'm sorry,
I didn't do it on purpose
Now I've made a mess
on both the table
and your vest

I saw it splash on your chair
and heard you scream
"How Dare You, How Dare!"

It was an accident
Honest,
I didn't mean to do it
My wrist just bumped the glass
Yes, I know I'm stupid

At least it wasn't
completely full, right?
Do you have to make
your fist so tight?

Yes, I know
you had to hit me
as hard as you could

I know you think
that will do me some good

You certainly believe it should

Your father knew for you it would

Don’t worry
if along the way
it may mold me to be mean
I’ll be gone from here
and from you
the day I turn fifteen

I realize you’re still mad
but it happened over an hour ago
Dad,
Can’t we just let it go?
I know,
I know

If you didn’t have us
to put up with
your life would be much better
You could do what you want
all the time
and you’d have more
than that dime,
the one you keep talking about
that you don’t have

Okay
I’ll leave you alone,
I just thought
you might want to talk
or take a walk
around the block
with me

so I could try to apologize
one more time

Strutters

She's got the look
She's dressed to kill
Her eyes say 'E Ticket'
then ask rhetorically, while sliding aside
Interested?
Wanna ride?

Her walk says thrill
Her glare says chill
Her perpetual come-on screams
"I will"
but her attitude informs;
no limitless credit cards
then my friend
you can count on nil

Believing she's ideal,
surreal
Long term possibilities
we don't consider
It's an enviable trophy
and eye-candy piece on our arms
with imagined head pleasures
causing us to jitter

All flash
no substance,
most men don't care
Women point out unabashedly
"one can't have it all,
if there's nothing there"

Plastic procedures
falsifications galore
some double digit
if we're keeping score

Man says "I see
and know it to be
but none of that matters
or bothers me
As long as I can
fawn my Madonna
and later, fondle my whore"

"Does she do the nasty?"
"They all do, eventually"
Only one question remains;
what her price will be?

What will it cost you
to have lust, sex and love
with vamps and vixens
Those self-indulged vultures
posing as doves

your future
your potential
your self respect
your good name,
your position
your power
your play in the game

your reputation
your new wife
your future wife
your home
your family. . .
your life?

What will it cost you
to stroke her ego daily
Insuring she never tires
leaving you full of doubt
and self-flagellatingly crazy

We asked our expert
about those faux beauties
who are always
struttin',
showin'
hot airin'
and attitude blowin'

"Trust me" he said,
a twinkle in his eye
"There is one thing
none can escape
No matter who they be
nor what may be tried,
or how many times
they attempt to expense it"

"For each and every
Virtually all inevitably
and hence undeniably,
the years and gravity
will override surgical propensities"

"Why jump through hoops
and beat yourself up
to be with one
whose first and only
interest in life
is in the mirror
on the wall,
overwhelmed by insecure attempts
to be the fairest of all"

"I've known a 'Cosmo' or two
a number of pros and back street hookers
Some with money
Others poor as church mice"

"But of the lot
those without the runway ego's
are always nice
and deliciously hot"

He continued explaining
"If I had my choice
who would it be?
The plain and everyday Jane's
or all those others
trapped in their own hype?"

"Why waste your good time
energies and efforts
Why waste your life
on saccharin and plastic,
when those mature and secure
are always fantastic"

Tattoo

A little pain
not too much

Permanent stain
you can touch

It won't rub off
with wash or scrub
Takes a laser beam to remove
the indelible longevity
of a momentary escape
to mental levity

Once as lonely
and unique
as a long haired Bob Seger
with his Silver Bullet Band
traveling on the roads
across C & W land

As they bad mouthed
ridiculed and glibly harassed
his hair length and style
Now to find one shorn
Nashville music man
you'd need to search
a country mile

Same with all
those ink tattoos
Once unique
on relative few
Now there are multiples
of colors, shapes
and designs
found on every one or two

Tethered

I can't imagine what else there is to live for
What singular episode
around the corner of tomorrow
would be so enticing
as to merit wishing or hoping
for one more day

The experience of lying down each night
envelopes my psyche
the way the sheets do my exhausted limbs
Relaxation, Desensitization
to a point of mimicking a bodily implosion

To wake once again rested,
until I rise and stumble onward
into another new day

My spirit lives
as my body dies
My soul waits to be freed
from the physical confines
tethering it
to this claustrophobic reality
called life

The Box

An ancient box
once commissioned
to be constructed and suitable
Precise detailing
a dwelling place
to house
the uncontainable

Specific plans called for
nay, demanded
pure gold and acacia wood
with workmanship
to be the best
far beyond very good

When finished it would go
before its tribal followers
Declaring to a conflicted world
benefits of sin resistance
and the blessings of obedience

Containing selected items
special to Him for us
Evidence of His words and wishes
that merit all our trust

Somewhere along the way
from one era unto the next
this box was taken
stolen or lost,
it's unavailability to all mankind
an enormous mounting cost

After thirty-four hundred
or so odd years
eclipsing and passing on
Questions as to its whereabouts
No, its very existence
Be it known or be it shown
could settle many a score
would open many a door

Perhaps one day in the future
Exactly when still unknown
this daunting mystery
be solved and then,
evidence of His relationship sown

Where has the box been kept?
Where was it taken or sent?
When will it be revealed again?
This Ark of the Covenant

Vegas Run

How fitting
it should end here,
in Vegas
where it all started

You walking away
how symbolic,
already gone
in your mind
your non-hesitant gait
one step short of a run

As if the years might fade
like a mirage
in this desert's heat
as you travel
further
from what was once
your oasis

There is no escape
from your indifference,
the past
stalks each of us
as closely
as a shadow

Wall Flower

Another Junior High Dance
sitting, waiting
hoping someone will,
praying no one does,
ask me to dance

I've been practicing at home
in front of the mirror
with my mother and little sis
Trying to get the steps right
in tempo, in sequence

There goes Cindy
she's such a show off
If I had a big sister
I'd know what to say
and the best way
to sweep back my hair
effortlessly
with the swish of my head

Why do I have to be here tonight?
Everyone is having such a good time,
Except the four of us sitting here
Four alone, together

Side glances between us
waiting to see
who may be first
if at all,
and God forbid
who may be last
or worse,
left sitting here
alone and cursed
while everyone else
is dancing

Oh my God!
Here comes Charles the Geek
He's coming straight at us
Oh no, he's going to ask
one of us to dance
Oh no, he's heading
for Linda, on my left
Oh no, he's about to ask

Oh yes Charles,
I'd love to dance with you

We Three

I was alone
in this universe whole
my desire, your presence
before my throne
for I AM God
and my choice was never
to be on my own

to be one with me
and see my face
each must inhabit
my sin free space

not a singular fleck
not one little speck
of sin
in my holy presence may there be
and it is this that keeps each
separated from me

that you and I may be near
I have sent to you myself
my spirit dwelling within a form
humanity could recognize,
a few with your hearts
but most with your eyes

for he is, as I AM
the same spirit are we
purity did temporarily reside
in your den of sin
that each of you fully stained
might yet live again

my unconditional love was for him
as his is now for you,
through this love
both you and he
may now stand together
before me

for he was sinless pure
and put it aside
to redeem you and yours,
he took your penalty
paid the price
suffering death in your place

the manner by which
you come to me
is through my spirit given free,
to acquire said
to accept and join us
is in my son to believe;
that he is of me
that we are one
serving you
in the form of three

I’ve made it simple
for all to see
how easy it is
to be one with me
eternally

Youth

Youth believes it has a wealth of knowledge.
Misinterpreting in actuality
that it possesses no depth of experience,
the young don't realize they are young

a singular plane
existing within a three dimensional reality
their gaze is focused, pinpointed,
avoiding the plethora of variables
waiting patiently to steal their dreams and hopes
through disillusionment produced by failure

unable to see beyond
a particular moment's self fulfillment
conditional ignorance makes prey
of what would otherwise be innocence

attempts to preempt
nature's nurturing ways
circumvents life's lessons
in a rush of exemplary judgment
which sidesteps relational cause and effect,
thrusting the young into dens of inequity
to be devoured by the jaws of predatory man
from which no past may be reclaimed

it is in their enigmatic pursuits
they discover the persistence necessary
for the rebirth of progress,
that future woes begotten by their numbers
are buffered and layered
beneath veils of convenience
as they live out lives of quiet desperation

Story teller Branch Isole is the author of nine books. Born in Osaka, Japan, Branch traveled extensively growing up, calling many places home. Finishing high school in Southern California he went on to graduate from Texas State University, attended graduate school at the University of Houston and received an M.A. degree from Trinity Theological Seminary.

Branch Isole is the Voyeuristic Poet.
His catalogue of work includes books, greeting cards and inspirational gift mats, all available at www.manaopublishing.com

Other books by Branch Isole
Messages In A Bottle ©
Inspirations in Poetic Prose
ISBN 978-0974769295

Postcards from the Line of Demarcation ©
Points of Separation in Poetic Prose
ISBN 978-0974769264

Reflections On Chrome ©
Parking Lot Confessions in Poetic Prose
ISBN 978-0974769257

Seeds of Mana'o ©
Thoughts, Ideas and Opinions in Poetic Prose
ISBN 978-0974769219

Barking Geckos ©
Stories and Observations in Poetic Prose
ISBN 978-0974769226

Crucibles ©
Refinement of the Neophyte Christian
ISBN 978-0974769233

Power of Praise ©
Poetry of Spiritual Christianity ™
ISBN 978-0974769271

GOD. . .i believe ©
Simple Steps on the Path
of Spiritual Christianity ™
ISBN 978-0974769202

www.ingramcontent.com/pod-product-compliance
Lightning Source LLC
La Vergne TN
LVHW090959080826
845145LV00003B/1062

* 9 7 8 0 9 7 4 7 6 9 2 8 8 *